Bond

STRETCH
Maths
Tests and Papers

8–9 years

Paul Broadbent

Nelson Thornes

Published in 2013 by:
Nelson Thornes Ltd
Delta Place
27 Bath Road
CHELTENHAM
GL53 7TH
United Kingdom

13 14 15 16 17 / 10 9 8 7 6 5 4 3 2 1

A catalogue record for this book is available from the British Library

ISBN 978 1 4085 1875 5

Page make-up and illustrations by GreenGate Publishing Services, Tonbridge, Kent

Printed in China by 1010 Printing International Ltd

Introduction

What is Bond?

The Bond *Stretch* series is a new addition to the Bond range of assessment papers, the number one series for the 11+, selective exams and general practice. Bond *Stretch* is carefully designed to challenge above and beyond the level provided in the regular Bond assessment range.

How does this book work?

The book contains two distinct sets of papers, along with full answers and a Progress Chart:

- Focus tests, accompanied by advice and directions, are focused on particular (and age-appropriate) Maths question types encountered in the 11+ and other exams, but devised at a higher level than the standard *Assessment Papers*. Each Focus test is designed to help raise a child's skills in the question type as well as offer plenty of practice for the necessary techniques.

- Mixed papers are full-length tests containing a full range of Maths question types. These are designed to provide rigorous practice for children working at a level higher than that required to pass at the 11+ and other Maths tests.

Full answers are provided for both types of test in the middle of the book.

Some questions may require a ruler or protractor. Calculators are not permitted.

How much time should the tests take?

The tests are for practice and to reinforce learning, and you may wish to test exam techniques and working to a set time limit. We would recommend your child spends 60 minutes to answer the 50 questions in each Mixed paper.

You can reduce the suggested time by five minutes to practise working at speed.

Using the Progress Chart

The Progress Chart can be used to track Focus test and Mixed paper results over time to monitor how well your child is doing and identify any repeated problems in tackling the different question types.

Focus test 1 — Place value

Circle the fraction that is the same as each decimal number.

1 0.8 → 8 $\dfrac{8}{10}$ $\dfrac{8}{100}$ $\dfrac{8}{1000}$

2 0.07 → 7 $\dfrac{7}{10}$ $\dfrac{7}{100}$ $\dfrac{7}{1000}$

> Remember: putting a zero on the end of a decimal doesn't change the number. 1.2 is the same as 1.20 and 1.200

3 Answer these.

$0.4 \times 10 =$ _____ $1.83 \times 10 =$ _____ $19 \div 10 =$ _____ $2.7 \div 10 =$ _____

Write the number shown on each abacus.

4 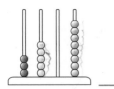 _____

5 _____

6 Write the number that is at each position.

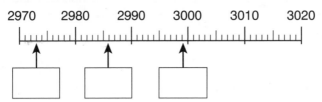

2970   2980   2990   3000   3010   3020

☐   ☐   ☐

In each group of numbers, circle the smallest number and underline the largest number.

7 4621   4612   4162   4261   8 8400   8404   8044   8440

9 Write this set of decimals in order to make the number statement correct.

2.7   7.02   7.2   2.72

_____ < _____ < _____ < _____

10 These are the lengths of four of the longest rivers in the world.
Round each to the nearest 100 km.

River name	Amazon	Congo	Mississippi	Nile
Length	6387 km	4371 km	6270 km	6690 km
Round to nearest 100 km	_____	_____	_____	_____

1 Complete these calculations.

```
  2 8 . 6
  1 7 . 4
+   9 . 2
_____
```

```
  6 5 0 3
- 2 8 7 9
_____
```

> Always estimate an approximate answer and then check your answer with the estimate at the end.

2 In Year 5 there are two classes. One has 29 pupils. The other has 32 pupils. On Wednesday there were 4 children away from each class.

How many children were there in the Year in total on Wednesday?

_____

3 I'm thinking of a number. If I halve the number and then add 8 the answer is 30.

What number am I thinking of? _____

4 What is the difference between 28.5 and 35.2? _____

5 The cost of a holiday is £285 in April and £445 in July.

What is the difference in cost between the two months? _____

6 Write the missing digits, 1, 2 and 3, in this calculation.

```
  □ 8 □
+ 4 4 9
_____
  6 □ 1
```

7 Add each row and column to find the figure in the bottom right-hand corner.

38	94	
72	43	

8 Join each pair of numbers that has a difference of 25.

47   53   38   37

62   63   72   28

9 What is the total weight of two boxes weighing 4.5 kg and 8.6 kg? _____

10 Jake has some 20p and 10p coins. He has three more 10p coins than 20p coins and altogether he has £1.50.

How many of each coin does he have?

_____ 10p coins and _____ 20p coins

Multiplication and division

1 Use each of the digits to complete the multiplications.

2　　**3**　　**4**　　**5**　　**6**　　**7**

__ × __ = 24　　　　__ × __ = 15　　　　__ × __ = 14

2 Write = , < or > to make each statement true.

57 ÷ 3 __ 19　　　　9 × 8 __ 68　　　　54 ÷ 6 __ 12

3 This is a 'multiply by 6' machine. Write the missing numbers in the chart.

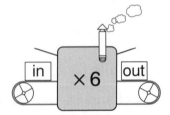

IN	7	3	__	6	__
OUT	42	__	54	__	24

For this grid method multiply each pair of numbers to complete the grid. Then add up each row and find the total.

4 What is 56 multiplied by 28?

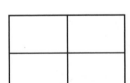

×

Total: _____

Example: What is 37 multiplied by 45?

×	30	7	
40	1200	280	1480
5	150	35	185

Total: 1665

5 Write in the missing number.　　24 × __ = 480

6 What is 743 divided by 5?

$$\begin{array}{r} \overline{}\ r\ \underline{} \\ 5\overline{)\,7\,4\,3} \end{array}$$

7 A recipe makes 12 cakes each weighing 150 g.

What is the total weight of cakes made using this recipe? _____

8 David wants to buy a bike costing £92. He saves £8 a week.

How many weeks will he need to save before he can buy the bike?

_____

9 Which number between 40 and 50 has a remainder of 2 when it is divided by 6? _____

10 Sam eats five cereal bars each week. There are eight bars in a pack.

How many packs are needed to last Sam for six weeks? _____

Now go to the Progress Chart to record your score!   Total ◯ 10

Focus test 4   Multiples and factors

1 Circle the numbers that are multiples of 4.

24   30   56   80   62   54   84   75   63

2 Write each of these four numbers in the correct place on the Venn diagram.

21   32   25   30

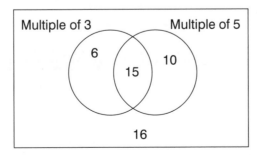

Multiple of 3   Multiple of 5

6

15   10

16

3 Ali says 'Only numbers ending in 5 are multiples of 5.'

Is he correct? Circle the answer: **yes**   **no**

Explain how you know.

_____

4 Write any multiple of 6 greater than 40. _____

5 What is the smallest number that is a multiple of both 4 and 10? _____

Factors are those numbers that will divide exactly into other numbers. It is useful to put factors of numbers into pairs:

Factors of 15   →   (1, 15)   (3, 5)   15 has four factors.

---

6 Here are all the pairs of factors for a number.

Write the number and complete the first pair of factors.

_____ → (1, _____)   (2, 12)   (3, 8)   (4, 6)

7 Write the missing factors for 18.

18 → (1, _____)   (2, _____)   (3, _____)

8 Put a circle around the numbers that are factors of 21.

     7   5   9   4   3   2   11

9 Which of these numbers are factors of 60? _____ and _____

     12   18   9   15   24   7

10 Write all the pairs of factors for each of these numbers.

      20   **12**

(_____ , _____)   (_____ , _____)

(_____ , _____)   (_____ , _____)

(_____ , _____)   (_____ , _____)

Focus test 5 Fractions, decimals and percentages

1 What fraction of this shape is shaded?

Circle the answer.

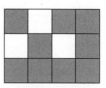

$$\frac{1}{4} \qquad \frac{1}{3} \qquad \frac{2}{3} \qquad \frac{3}{4}$$

2 Put a tick in each row to complete this table.

	Greater than $\frac{1}{2}$	Less than $\frac{1}{2}$
0.35		
0.55		
0.25		
0.05		

3 Complete these equivalent fraction chains.

$$\frac{3}{4} = \frac{\square}{8} = \frac{9}{\square} = \frac{\square}{\square}$$

$$\frac{2}{3} = \frac{4}{\square} = \frac{\square}{9} = \frac{\square}{\square}$$

4 Write < , > or = between each pair of fractions.

$$\frac{2}{5} \; \text{---} \; \frac{3}{10} \qquad\qquad \frac{1}{2} \; \text{---} \; \frac{3}{6} \qquad\qquad \frac{3}{4} \; \text{---} \; \frac{7}{8}$$

5 Match each of these fraction calculations to its answer.

$\frac{1}{3}$ of 27

$\frac{1}{5}$ of 40

$\frac{1}{8}$ of 32

4

6

8

9

5

10

6 Write these fractions in order, starting with the smallest.

$$\frac{2}{5} \qquad \frac{7}{20} \qquad \frac{1}{2} \qquad \frac{3}{10}$$

_____

> Percentages are fractions out of 100. That's what per cent means: out of 100.
>
> % is the percentage sign.

7 What percentage of this pattern is shaded? _____

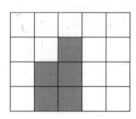

8 Write these fractions as percentages.

$$\frac{3}{10} \text{ \_\_\_\_} \qquad \frac{1}{2} \text{ \_\_\_\_} \qquad \frac{1}{4} \text{ \_\_\_\_}$$

9 What is 75% as a fraction? Circle the answer.

$$\frac{7}{50} \qquad \frac{1}{4} \qquad \frac{3}{4} \qquad \frac{3}{25}$$

10 Write these percentages as fractions.

10% _____   60% _____   80% _____

Now go to the Progress Chart to record your score! Total ◯ 10

If you need to find missing numbers in a sequence, look carefully at the numbers you are given. Try to work out the numbers next to these first, and then write the others.

1 What is the next number in this sequence?

67   64   61   58   _____

2 What is the missing number in this sequence? Circle the answer.

9   16   25   _____   49   64

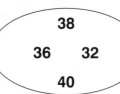

38

36   32

40

Write the missing numbers in these sequences.

3 _67_   78   89   100   _____   122

4 540   _____   _____   390   340   290

5 0.3   0.6   _____   _____   1.5   1.8

In these sequences each number is double the previous number.

Write the missing numbers.

6 _____   _____   4   8   16   _____   _____

7 _____   _____   100   200   400   _____   _____

8 What is the next square number in this sequence?

25   36   49   _____

Look at these number patterns. Write the next two numbers in each sequence.

9 9038   9036   9034   9032   _____   _____

10 2976   2981   2986   2991   2996   _____   _____

Now go to the Progress Chart to record your score!   Total   ◯   10

11

1 Write the letters for each shape in the correct position on the Carroll diagram.

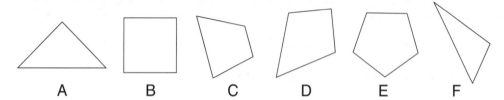

A   B   C   D   E   F

	Symmetrical	Not symmetrical
Quadrilateral	_____	_____
Not a quadrilateral	_____	_____

2 Tick the right-angled triangle.

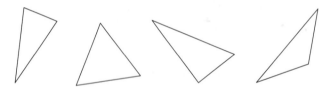

3 Sort these shapes into prisms and pyramids. Tick the correct box in the table for each shape.

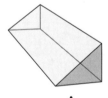
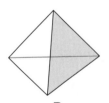
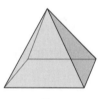

A   B   C   D

	A	B	C	D
Pyramid				
Prism				

4 Draw a quadrilateral on this grid.
It must only have one pair of parallel sides and two right angles.

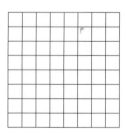

5 Tick the chart to show whether each angle is acute, obtuse or right-angled.

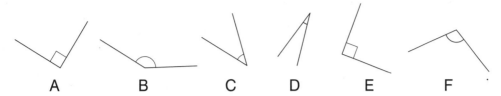

A   B   C   D   E   F

	A	B	C	D	E	F
Acute						
Obtuse						
Right-angled						

6 The dashed line is a mirror line. Shade more squares to show the reflection of the L-shape in the mirror line.

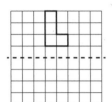

When a mirror is put on a line of symmetry the half shape and its reflection show the whole shape.

Write the name of each shape that is described.

7 Which shape has 6 faces, 12 edges and 8 vertices? _____

8 Which shape has 5 faces, 8 edges and 5 vertices? _____

9 Which shape has 5 faces, 9 edges and 6 vertices? _____

10 Draw lines on this shape so that it would make a cube if you folded it. Use a ruler to measure where the lines go.

Focus test 8 — Area and perimeter

1 What is the approximate area of the shaded shape? Circle the correct answer.

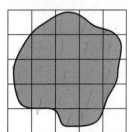

25 squares   15 squares

12 squares   20 squares

2 What are the area and perimeter of this rectangle?

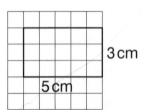

3 cm

5 cm

Area = _____

Perimeter = _____

> To find the area of a rectangle multiply the length by the width.
>
> Example:
>
>
>
> 3 cm
>
> 4 cm
>
> Area = 3 cm × 4 cm = 12 square centimetres

3 Draw a rectangle with an area of 18 square centimetres.

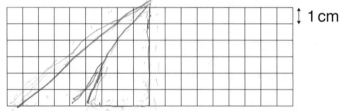

↕ 1 cm

Calculate the area and perimeter of each of these rectangles.

8 cm

3 cm

5 cm

7 cm

4 Area = _____

Perimeter = _____

5 Area = _____

Perimeter = _____

6 A rectangle has an area of 24 square centimetres and a perimeter of 20 cm.
Draw the rectangle on this square grid.

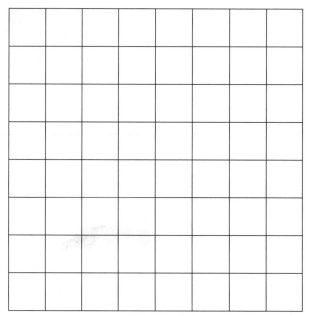

7 What is the perimeter of this shape?

_____

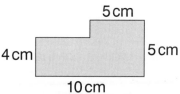

8 The area of this square is 16 square centimetres.

What is the length of each side?

_____

9 What is the area of a square tile with a 12 cm side?

_____

12 cm

10 A farmer wants to put a length of electric wire round a field to keep in his sheep. The field is 50 m by 80 m.

What length electric wire will he need? _____

Focus test 9　Measures

It is important to write the units in your answers, for example cm, ml or g.

1 Circle the correct measure for each of these items.

My drink bottle holds → 33 litres　　30 ml　　330 ml　　3 ml

A plum weighs → 9 g　　90 g　　9 kg　　90 kg

2 Write this set of measures in length order, starting with the smallest.

20 cm　　　220 mm　　　20 mm　　　2 m

_____

3 Answer each of these questions.

How many millilitres are there in three litres? _____

How many grams are there in two and a half kilograms? _____

How many metres are there in one and a half kilometres? _____

4 Use a ruler to measure the length of side a.

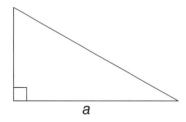

a

Give your answer in millimetres. _____

5 How much liquid is in this jug? _____

500 ml
400 ml
300 ml
200 ml
100 ml
0

6 Draw an arrow on this scale to show 750 grams.

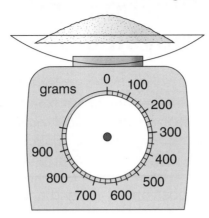

This clock shows the time when a TV programme ended.

7 At what time did the programme finish? _____

8 The programme lasted 55 minutes.

At what time did it start? _____

9 These shapes weigh 32 kg altogether.

If each cube weighs 4 kg, what is the weight of each sphere?

_____

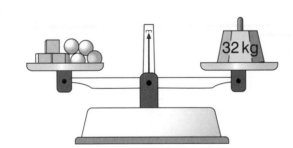

32 kg

10 What is the difference in the amount of liquid in these two jugs?

_____

Focus test 10 Position and movement

When you write coordinates, the number on the horizontal x-axis is written first, followed by the number on the vertical y-axis. You can remember this because x comes before y in the alphabet.

1–3 Plot each point in the correct position on the grid and label it with its letter.

A (4, 5)

B (0, 6)

C (2, 3)

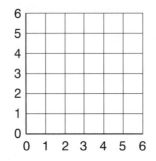

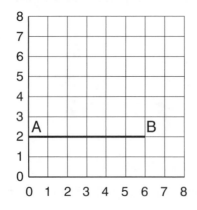

4 Circle the coordinates of point A. (2, 0) (0, 0) (0, 2) (6, 2)

5 Write the coordinates of point B. (____ , ____)

6 Draw a cross at (7, 6) and label it C. Draw a cross at (1, 6) and label it D.

7 Join the points ABCD and then join D to A. What is the name of the shape you have drawn? ______________

8 Label the arrows pointing south, west and east with the letters S, W and E.

9 Label the arrows pointing SW, NE, NW and SE.

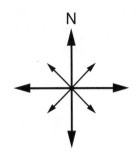

10 Complete this chart to show where you would be facing after each turn.

Start position, facing	Turn	End position, now facing
North	$\frac{1}{4}$ turn anticlockwise	_____
South	$\frac{1}{2}$ turn clockwise	_____
West	$\frac{1}{4}$ turn anticlockwise	_____
East	$\frac{1}{4}$ turn clockwise	_____

Now go to the Progress Chart to record your score!   Total ⬤ 10

This bar chart shows the number of ice creams sold on each day in one week.

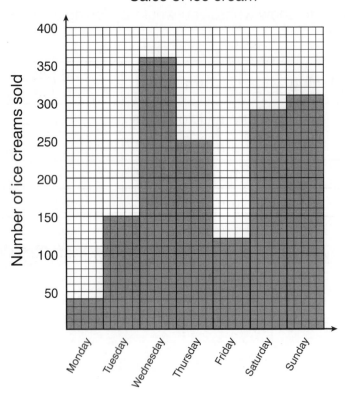

Sales of ice cream

1 How many ice creams were sold on Friday? _____

2 On which day were 250 ice creams sold? _____

3 There was one very hot day. Which day do you think was very hot?

_____

4 How many more ice creams were sold on Sunday than Saturday?

_____

5 How many ice creams were sold altogether on Monday and Tuesday?

_____

This bar chart shows the number of books that were taken out from a school library and returned to the library each day of a week.

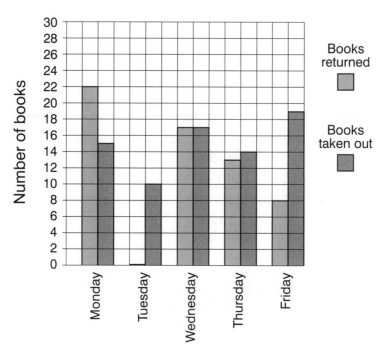

School library books record

Number of books (y-axis): 0, 2, 4, 6, 8, 10, 12, 14, 16, 18, 20, 22, 24, 26, 28, 30

Days of the week: Monday, Tuesday, Wednesday, Thursday, Friday

Books returned

Books taken out

6 On which day were the most books taken out of the library?

_____

7 On which day were no books brought back to the library?

_____

8 How many more books were taken out than brought back on Friday?

_____

9 On which day was the same number of books taken out and brought back? _____

10 What was the total number of books taken out and brought back on Thursday? _____

Venn diagrams and Carroll diagrams

1–4 Write each of these numbers in the correct place on the Carroll diagram. Four numbers have been done for you.

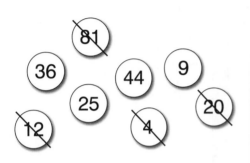

	Multiple of 3	Not a multiple of 3
Square number	81	4
Not a square number	12	20

5 Write each number from 1 to 15 in the correct place on the Venn diagram. Four numbers have been done for you.

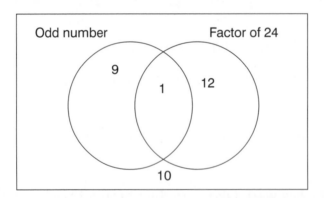

The top left section of a Carroll diagram matches the intersecting set of a Venn diagram that has the same information. The other sections of each diagram can also be matched.

	Odd number	Not an odd number
Factor of 24	1	12
Not a factor of 24	9	10

6–9 Draw each shape in the correct position on the Carroll diagram.

	Symmetrical	Not symmetrical
Has one or more right angles		
Has no right angles		

10 Write the letters for each shape in the correct position on the Venn diagram.

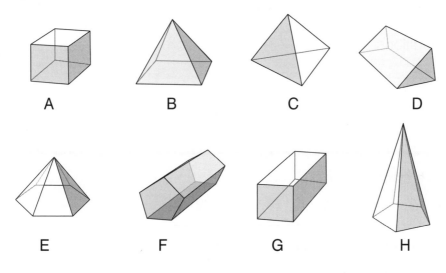

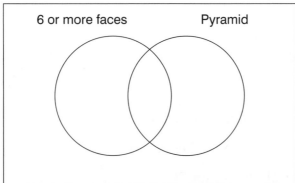

Mixed paper 1

1–3 Write the number that is at each position on the number line.

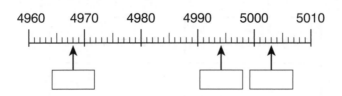

4 Write the number shown on the abacus. _____

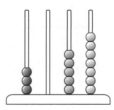

Complete these additions.

5
```
  5 8 6 9
+   3 7 3
---------

---------
```

6
```
  7 7 0 4
+ 1 6 9 8
---------

---------
```

7 What is 901 take away 552? _____

8 What is the difference between 178 and 4022? _____

Write = , < or > to make each statement true.

9 3×6 ___ 5×4

10 6×4 ___ 8×3

11 $15 \div 5$ ___ $16 \div 4$

12 $30 \div 6$ ___ $32 \div 8$

13–14 Circle the two numbers that are a multiple of 3.

16   27   32   47   53   74   84

15–16 Write the missing pair of factors for 30.

30 → (1, 30) (2, 15) (3, 10) (__ , __)

3

1

2

2

4

2

2

Any answer that requires units of measurement should be marked wrong if the correct units have not been included.

Focus test 1

1. $\frac{8}{10}$
2. $\frac{7}{100}$
3. 4, 18.3, 1.9, 0.27
4. 3508
5. 6745
6. 2973, 2986, 2999
7. 4162 *circled*, 4621 *underlined*
8. 8044 *circled*, 8440 *underlined*
9. **2.7** < **2.72** < **7.02** < **7.2**
10. 6400 km, 4400 km, 6300 km, 6700 km

Focus test 2

1. 55.2, 3624
2. 53
3. 44
4. 6.7
5. £160
6.

	1	8	2
+	4	4	9
6	3	1	

7.

38	94	**132**
72	43	**115**
110	137	247

8. 47 and 72, 53 and 28, 38 and 63, 37 and 62
9. 13.1 kg
10. 7 × 10p, 4 × 20p coins

Focus test 3

1. **4** × **6** = 24, **3** × **5** = 15, **2** × **7** = 14
2. 57 ÷ 3 = **19**, 9 × 8 **>** 68, 54 ÷ 6 **<** 12
3.

IN	7	3	**9**	6	**4**
OUT	42	**18**	54	**36**	24

Focus test 4

1. 24, 56, 80, 84
2.

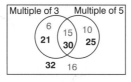

Multiple of 3 — Multiple of 5: 6, 21, 15, 30 | 10, 25
32, 16

3. No, numbers ending in 0 are also multiples of 5 because they are multiples of 10, and 10 is a multiple of 5.
4. *Check answer is a multiple of 6 and greater than 40. Possible answers are:* 42, 48, 54, 60, 66, 72, 78, 84, 90, 96, 102, 108
5. 20
6. 24, 24
7. 18, 9, 6
8. 7, 3
9. 12 and 15
10. 20 (1, 20) (2, 10) (4, 5)
    12 (1, 12) (2, 6) (3, 4)

Focus test 5

1. $\frac{3}{4}$
2.

	Greater than $\frac{1}{2}$	Less than $\frac{1}{2}$
0.35		✓
0.55	✓	
0.25		✓
0.05		✓

3. $\frac{3}{4} = \frac{6}{8} = \frac{9}{12} = \frac{12}{16}$
   $\frac{2}{3} = \frac{4}{6} = \frac{6}{9} = \frac{8}{12}$
4. $\frac{2}{5}$ **>** $\frac{3}{10}$
   $\frac{1}{2}$ **=** $\frac{3}{6}$
   $\frac{3}{4}$ **<** $\frac{7}{8}$
5. $\frac{1}{3}$ of 27 → **9**
   $\frac{1}{5}$ of 40 → **8**
   $\frac{1}{8}$ of 32 → **4**
6. $\frac{3}{10}, \frac{7}{20}, \frac{2}{5}, \frac{1}{2}$
7. 25%
8. 30%, 50%, 25%
9. $\frac{3}{4}$
10. $\frac{1}{10}, \frac{6}{10}$ *or* $\frac{3}{5}, \frac{8}{10}$ *or* $\frac{4}{5}$

Focus test 6

1. 55
2. 36
3. 67, 111
4. 490, 440
5. 0.9, 1.2
6. 1, 2, 32, 64
7. 25, 50, 800, 1600
8. 64
9. 9030, 9028
10. 3001, 3006

Focus test 7

1.

	Symmetrical	Not symmetrical
Quadrilateral	B, D	C
Not a quadrilateral	A, E	F

2.

3.

	A	B	C	D
Pyramid		✓	✓	
Prism	✓			✓

4. *Any trapezium that has 2 parallel sides and 2 right angles. This is one possible answer:*

Focus test 4 (answer 4 table — right column)

5.

	A	B	C	D	E	F
Acute			✓	✓		
Obtuse		✓				✓
Right-angled	✓				✓	

6.

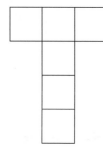

7. cuboid
8. pyramid *or* square-based pyramid
9. prism *or* triangular prism
10.

Focus test 8

1. 15 squares
2. Area = 15 square centimetres, Perimeter = 16 centimetres
3. *One of the following rectangles:* 2 × 9, 3 × 6, 1 × 18
4. Area = 24 square centimetres, Perimeter = 22 centimetres
5. Area = 35 square centimetres, Perimeter = 24 centimetres
6. *Check that a 6 cm × 4 cm rectangle has been drawn.*

(Answer 4 — top of second column)

4.

×	50	6	
20	1000	120	1120
8	400	48	448
		Total:	1568

5. 20
6. 148 r 3
7. 1800 g *or* 1.8 kg *or* 1 kg 800 g
8. 12 weeks
9. 44
10. 4 packs

7 30 cm
8 4 cm
9 144 square centimetres
10 260 m

Focus test 9

1 330 ml, 90 g
2 20 mm, 20 cm, 220 mm, 2 m
3 3000 ml, 2500 g, 1500 m
4 45 mm
5 350 ml
6

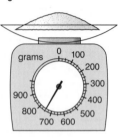

7 6:35
8 5:40
9 5 kg
10 50 ml

Focus test 10

1–3

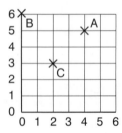

4 (0, 2)
5 (6, 2)
6

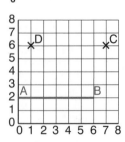

7 parallelogram

8

9

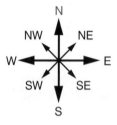

10

Start position, facing	Turn	End position, now facing
North	$\frac{1}{4}$ turn anti-clockwise	**West**
South	$\frac{1}{2}$ turn clockwise	**North**
West	$\frac{1}{4}$ turn anti-clockwise	**South**
East	$\frac{1}{4}$ turn clockwise	**South**

Focus test 11

1 120
2 Thursday
3 Wednesday
4 20
5 190
6 Friday
7 Tuesday
8 11
9 Wednesday
10 27

Focus test 12

1–4

	Multiple of 3	Not a multiple of 3
Square number	81 36 **9**	4 **25**
Not a square number	12	20 **44**

5

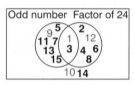

6–9

	Symmetrical	Not symmetrical
Has one or more right angles		
Has no right angles		

10

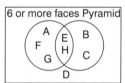

Mixed paper 1

1–3 4968, 4994, 5003
4 3057
5 6242
6 9402
7 349
8 3844
9 <
10 =
11 <
12 >
13–14 27, 84
15–16 (5, 6)
17 $\frac{2}{3}$
18 $\frac{30}{45}$
19 3
20 5
21 $\frac{1}{3}$
22–23 64, 67

24–25 4953, 4943
26 B
27 C
28 A
29 D and E
30 4
31–32 Area = 63 square centimetres, Perimeter = 32 cm
33–34 Area = 32 square centimetres, Perimeter = 24 cm
35–38 7 cm, 71 mm, 1 m, 107 cm
39 (5, 3)
40 (0, 1)
41 15
42 cheese
43 10
44 12
45 7
46 2
47 Beth
48 6
49

50 south

Mixed paper 2

1–2 2379 circled, 3729 underlined
3–4 6001 circled, 6110 underlined
5 3548
6 3275
7 579
8 852
9 2705

10–13

IN	4	6	9	20	50
OUT	28	42	63	140	350

14 12
15 18
16 5
17 9
18 9
19 $2\frac{7}{10}$
20 $4\frac{1}{5}$ or $4\frac{2}{10}$
21 >
22 >
23 7.2
24 2404

25–26   79, 71
27

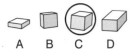

A   B   C   D

28

29 Angle **C** is an acute
    angle.

30

A   B   C

D   E   F

31 B
32 C
33 950 m
34 36 cm
35 10 g
36 10 litres
37 400 cm
38 3000 m
39–40

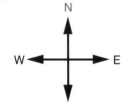

41–42

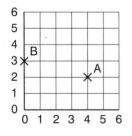

43 35 points
44 Omar
45 35
46 Sophia
47 2
48 May
49 4

50

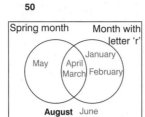

Spring month   Month with
                letter 'r'

May   April   January
      March   February
    August June

Mixed paper 3

1   $\frac{3}{10}$
2   $\frac{9}{100}$
3   15.2
4   3.4
5   23 cm
6   5.5 kg
7   5833
8   9153
9   95 g
10 £2.17
11 20
12 30
13 50
14–17

	A factor of 16	Not a factor of 16
A multiple of 4	**8**	**12**
Not a multiple of 4	**2**	**18**

18 >
19 <
20 =
21 =
22–23   583, 463
24–25   6, 96
26 C
27 square-based
    pyramid
28 isosceles
29 obtuse
30 6 m
31–32

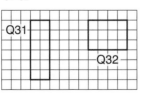

Q31   Q32

33 14 squares
34 150 ml
35 250 ml
36 100 ml
37 400 ml

38

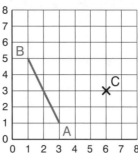

39 (3, 1)
40 (1, 5)
41 triangle
42 dog
43 fish
44 3
45 17
46–49

	Even number	Not an even number
Multiple of 7	28 **14**	7 **21**
Not a multiple of 7	16, 2, 26, 4, 18, 6, 20, 8, 10, 12, 22, 30, **24**	23, 15, 1, 3, 17, 27, 19, 5, 13, 29, 9, 25 **11**

50 13

Mixed paper 4

1–4   **5.08 < 5.85 < 8.5 < 80.5**
5   51.4
6   117.2
7   43.2
8   12.6
9   51
10 17
11 2052
12 238 r 1
13 false
14 true
15 18
16 60, 60
17–20 $\frac{1}{2}$ $\frac{11}{20}$ $\frac{3}{5}$ $\frac{9}{10}$
21 64
22–23   763, 755
24 100
25 sometimes
26 never
27 always
28 never
29 25 square metres
30 40 cm
31–32

33 86 mm
34 3:40
35 4:25
36 475 g
37–39

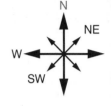

40–42

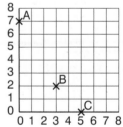

43 July
44 May
45 40 mm
46 7 months
47–50

Curved line   Line symmetry

J P   E H
Q S   B C   I K M
  G R   D O   T A
        U   V W X Y
      Z   F L N

	Length	Width	Area	Perimeter
Rectangle A	4 m	**5 m**	20 square metres	18 m
Rectangle B	3 m	**7 m**	21 square metres	20 m

Mixed paper 5

1. 9100
2. 9000
3. 9900
4. 10000
5. 6129
6. 6507
7. 39.1
8. 3230
9. 8.1
10. 1780
11. 486
12. 1424
13. 143
14. 3
15. 12
16. 42
17–18. 14, 7
19. $\frac{1}{4}$
20. $\frac{1}{5}$
21. 25%
22. 3
23–24. 15.1, 14.6
25–26. 7457, 8457
27. hexagon
28. 3
29. 0
30. 6
31. 22 m
32. 600 square centimetres
33–34. Area = 66 square metres, Perimeter = 34 m
35. 3 kg 500 g
36. 700 g
37. 3:20
38. 29 cm
39–42

Start position, facing	Turn	End position, now facing
East	$\frac{1}{4}$ turn anticlockwise	**North**
North	$\frac{1}{4}$ turn clockwise	**East**
East	$\frac{1}{2}$ turn clockwise	**West**
South	$\frac{1}{4}$ turn anticlockwise	**East**

43. 6
44. 5
45. 5
46. 42
47–50

	One or more acute angles	No acute angles
Quadrilateral	**A**	**D**
Not a quadrilateral	**C**	**B**

Mixed paper 6

1–4. 1876, 1901, 1929, 1993
5. 53 years
6. 86.4 m
7–9.

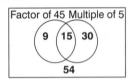

10. 36
11. yes
12. 975
13. 129 r 5
14–17.

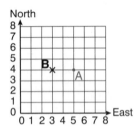

18–19. $\frac{5}{8}$, $\frac{3}{5}$
20. $\frac{2}{8}$
21. 0.75
22–23. 75, 1200
24. 4
25. 28

26–29.

	Odd number of vertices	Even number of vertices
One or more triangular faces	**A**	**B**
No triangular faces		**C, D**

30. 40 cm
31. 84 square centimetres
32. 108 square metres
33. 8 m
34–35. 5 ml *circled*, 50 litres *underlined*
36. 2500 g
37. 7 litres
38. (5, 4)
39.

North

8
7
6
5
4 B×   ·A
3
2
1
0
 0 1 2 3 4 5 6 7 8 East

40. west
41. true
42. 4
43. 2 children
44. 4 families
45. 18
46–49.

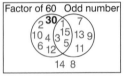

50.

Factor of 60   Odd number
2 **30** 1 7
10 4 3 15 13 9
6 12 5 5 11
  14 8

A4

Look at the rectangle to answer these questions.

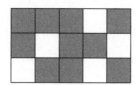

17 What fraction of this shape is shaded? Circle the answer.

$\frac{1}{2}$ $\frac{2}{3}$ $\frac{3}{4}$ $\frac{4}{5}$

18 Circle the fraction that is equivalent to the shaded part of this shape.

$\frac{15}{30}$ $\frac{20}{25}$ $\frac{30}{45}$ $\frac{15}{100}$

19 What is $\frac{1}{5}$ of 15? ___

20 What is $\frac{1}{3}$ of 15? ___

21 Which fraction is smaller, $\frac{2}{5}$ or $\frac{1}{3}$? ___

3

Write the next two numbers in each sequence.

22–23 52   55   58   61   _____   _____

24–25 4993   4983   4973   4963   _____   _____

Answer these questions using the letters A to E.

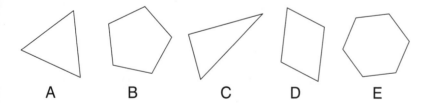

A   B   C   D   E

26 Which shape is a pentagon? _____

27 Which shape has a right angle? _____

28 Which shape has exactly three lines of symmetry? _____

29 Which two shapes have parallel sides? _____ and _____

30 How many lines of symmetry do squares have? _____

What are the area and perimeter of each of these rectangles?

31–32

9 cm

7 cm

Area = _____

Perimeter = _____

33–34

4 cm

8 cm

Area = _____

Perimeter = _____

4

35–38 Write these measures in order, starting with the smallest.

1 m   107 cm   71 mm   7 cm   _____ _____ _____ _____

smallest

4

39 Circle the coordinates of point A.

(0, 3)   (5, 0)   (3, 5)   (5, 3)   (3, 3)

40 What are the coordinates of point B?

(_____ , _____)

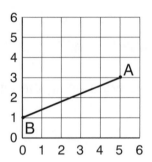

2

This pictogram shows the results of a survey on favourite pizza toppings.

🍕 = 5 people   🍕 = 1–4 people

Topping		
Ham	🍕 🍕 🍕	
Mushroom	🍕 🍕 🍕	
Cheese	🍕 🍕 🍕 🍕 🍕 🍕	
Tomato	🍕 🍕 🍕 🍕 🍕	

Favourite pizza toppings

41 How many people chose ham as their favourite pizza topping? _____

42 Which topping did 26–29 people choose as their favourite pizza topping? _____

43 How many more people preferred tomato to ham? _____

44 Circle the most likely number of people who chose mushroom as their favourite topping.

25        $2\frac{1}{2}$ 15   12

4

This Carroll diagram shows the shoes worn by a group of children.

Shoes	Laces	No laces
Black	Ali, Eve	Jack, Harry
Brown	Cara, Aidan, Haley, Ava, Emma	Beth

45 How many children are wearing shoes with laces? _____

46 How many children are wearing black shoes with laces? _____

47 Who is wearing brown shoes with no laces? _____

48 How many children are not wearing black shoes? _____

4

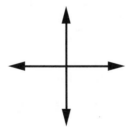

49 Label the arrow pointing north with an N.

50 If I faced north and made a half-turn clockwise, which direction would I be facing? Circle the answer.

     north   west   south   east

2

Now go to the Progress Chart to record your score!   Total   50

Mixed paper 2

In each group of numbers, circle the smallest number and underline the largest number.

1–2 2793   3297   2379   3729

3–4 6110   6001   6011   6101

4

A bakery has a café. These are the number of sandwiches and cakes that are bought to eat in or eat out in one week.

	Eat in	Eat out
Sandwiches	740	1319
Cakes	2808	1956

5 How many cakes and sandwiches in total were sold to eat in? _____

6 How many cakes and sandwiches in total were sold to eat out? _____

7 How many more sandwiches were sold to eat out than eat in? _____

8 How many more cakes were sold to eat in than eat out? _____

9 How many more cakes than sandwiches were sold in total? _____

5

10–13 This is a 'multiply by 7' machine. Write the missing numbers in the chart.

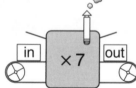

IN	4	_____	9	_____	50
OUT	28	42	_____	140	_____

4

Choose from these numbers to answer each question.

5   15   9   12   6   18

14 Which number is a multiple of 4? _____

15 Which number is a multiple of 9 and 3? _____

16 Which number is a factor of 70? _____

17 Which number is a factor of 63? _____

18 Which number is a square number? _____

5

Write these decimals as whole numbers and fractions.

19 2.7 → _____   **20** 4.2 → _____   2

Write < or > to make these statements true.

21 8.5 ___ $8\frac{1}{5}$ **22** $4\frac{3}{10}$ ___ $3\frac{4}{10}$ 2

23 What is the missing number in this sequence?

6.2   6.7 _____   7.7   8.2

24 What is the first number in this sequence?

_____   2409   2414   2419   2424

25–26 Write the missing numbers in this sequence.   4

95   87 _____ _____ 63   55

27 Circle the cube.

A   B   C   D

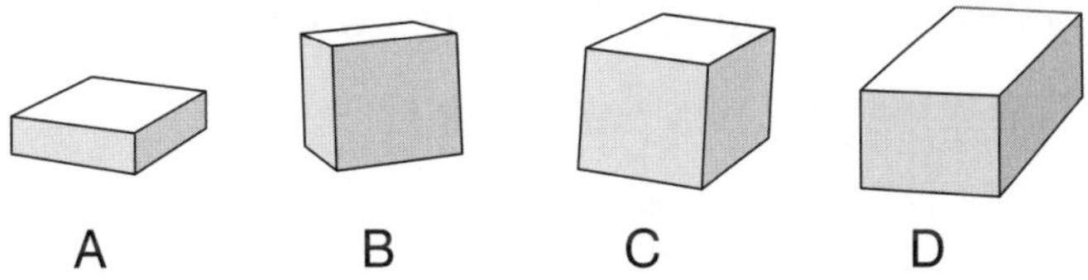

28 Draw a circle around each shape that is symmetrical.

2

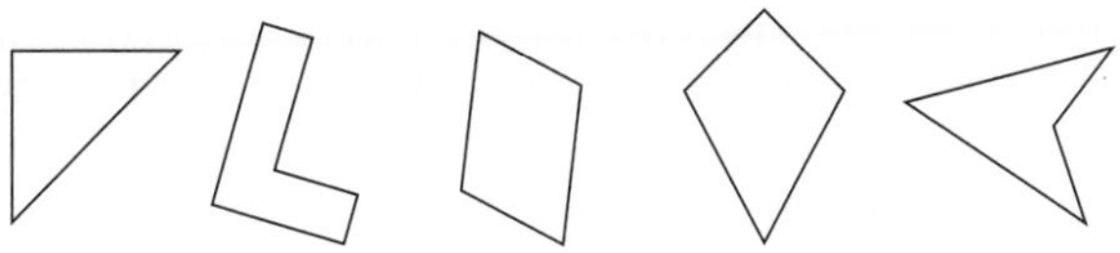

29 Look at this pentagon and write the letter of the correct angle to complete this statement.   1

Angle _____ is an acute angle.

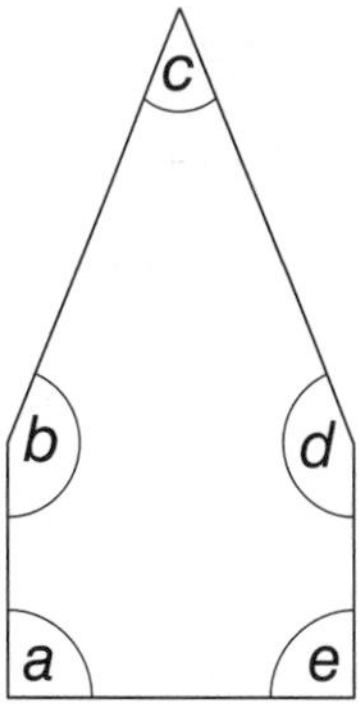

30 Draw a circle around each of the pyramids.

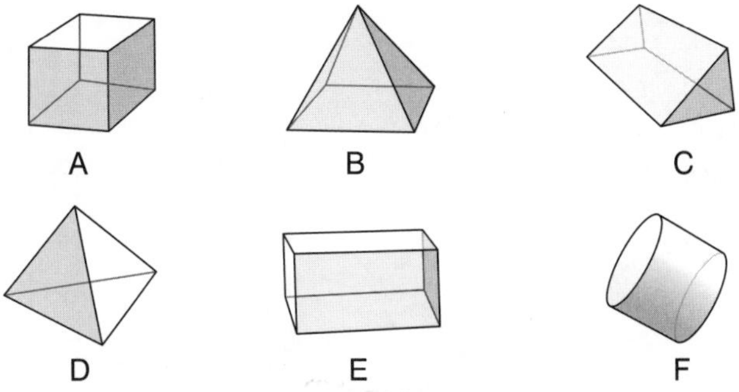

A   B   C

D   E   F

1

29

Look at these shapes and answer the questions.

5 cm

12 cm

A   3 cm

B   7 cm

9 cm

C   4 cm

31 Write the letter of the rectangle that does **not** have an area of 36 square centimetres. _____

32 Write the letter of the rectangle that has a perimeter of 26 cm. _____

33 A rectangular field has two sides each 350 m long. The other two sides are 125 m in length.

What is the total length of fencing that is needed to go around this field? _____

34 A square has an area of 81 square centimetres.

What is the length of its perimeter?

18 cm   9 cm   36 cm   49 cm

Circle the correct measure for each of these items.

35 A birthday card weighs → 10 g   500 g   1 kg   10 kg

36 A full bucket holds → 10 ml   500 ml   1 litre   10 litres

37 How many centimetres are there in 4 metres? _____ cm

38 How many metres are there in 3 kilometres? _____ m

39 Label the arrow pointing east with an E.

40 Label the arrow pointing west with a W.

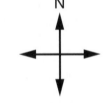

Plot each point in the correct position on the grid and label it with its letter.

41 A (4, 2)

42 B (0, 3)

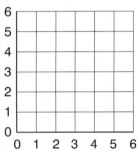

This graph shows the points scored by players on a Treasure Hunt game app.

43 How many points did Lily score? _____

44 Who scored 49 points? _____

45 What is the points difference between the player with the most points and the player with the fewest points? _____

46 Who scored four more points than Noel? _____

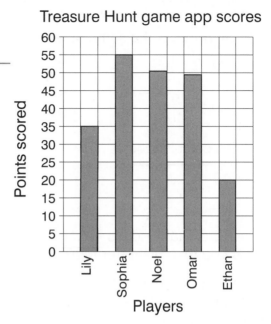

Treasure Hunt game app scores

4

The first six months of the year have been sorted on this Venn diagram.

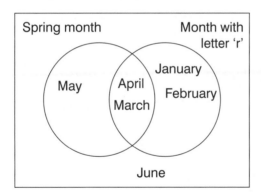

47 How many months have the letter 'r' and are in the spring? _____

48 Which month is in the spring but does not have the letter 'r' in it?

_____

49 How many months in the first half of the year have the letter 'r' in them? _____

50 Write **August** in the correct section on the Venn diagram.

4

Mixed paper 3

Circle the fraction that is the same as each decimal number.

1   0.3   3 $\dfrac{3}{10}$ $\dfrac{3}{100}$ $\dfrac{3}{1000}$

2   0.09   9 $\dfrac{9}{10}$ $\dfrac{9}{100}$ $\dfrac{9}{1000}$ (2)

Complete these calculations.

3   $1.52 \times 10 =$ _____

4   $34 \div 10 =$ _____   (2)

5   Lee is 162 cm tall and his younger sister Mia is 139 cm tall. How much taller is Lee than his sister Mia? _____

6   A shopping basket has a 2.55 kg bag of potatoes, a 1.75 kg box of washing powder and a 1.2 kg bag of onions. What is the total weight of shopping in this basket? _____   (2)

Look at these two numbers and answer the questions.

7493   1660

7   What is the difference between these two numbers? _____   (2)

8   What is the total when these two numbers are added together? _____   (2)

9   Three pizzas weigh 285 g. What is the weight of one pizza? _____

10   Individual pizzas cost 89p each. This 3-pack special offer is 50p cheaper than buying three individual pizzas. How much does the 3-pack special offer cost? _____   (2)

Write the missing numbers.

11   $13 \times$ __ $= 260$ 12 $180 \div$ __ $= 6$

13   $12 \times$ __ $= 600$ (3)

14–17 Write each of these numbers in the correct part of the Carroll diagram.

2	8	12	18

	A factor of 16	Not a factor of 16
A multiple of 4	_____	_____
Not a multiple of 4	_____	_____

○ 4

Write < , > or = between each pair.

18 $\dfrac{1}{2}$ ___ 0.25

19 $\dfrac{2}{5}$ ___ $\dfrac{5}{10}$

20 $\dfrac{1}{3}$ of 12 ___ $\dfrac{1}{2}$ of 8

21 40% ___ $\dfrac{4}{10}$

○ 4

Write the missing numbers in these sequences.

22–23 _____ 553 523 493 _____

24–25 _____ 12 24 48 _____

○ 4

26 Which of one these nets can be folded to make a cube?
Circle the correct letter.

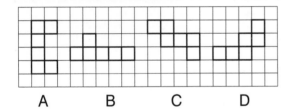

A   B   C   D

○ 1

27 Write the name of this shape. _____

Look at this triangle.

○ 1

28 What is the name of this triangle? Underline the answer.

equilateral   isosceles   right-angled   scalene

29 What type of angle is angle *y*? Underline the answer.

right angle   acute   obtuse

○ 2

30 The area of a square is 36 square metres.

What is the length of each side? _____

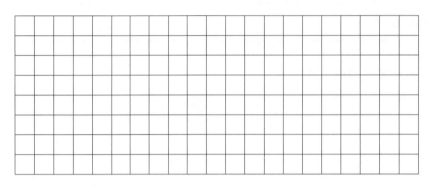

Draw two rectangles, each with an area of 12 square centimetres and these perimeters.

31 Perimeter = 16 cm

32 Perimeter = 14 cm

33 What is the area of this shape? Circle the answer.

8 squares

12 squares

14 squares

16 squares

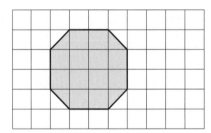

34–35 How much water is there in each jug?

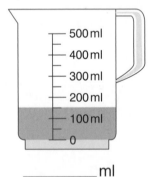

500 ml
400 ml
300 ml
200 ml
100 ml
0

1 litre

_____ ml   _____ ml

36 What is the difference in the amount of water between these two jugs?

_____

37 If the water from these two jugs were poured into one bottle, how much water would there be in total in the bottle? _____

1

2

1

4

38 Draw a cross at (6, 3) and label it C.

39 Write the coordinates for point A.

(_____ , _____)

40 Circle the coordinates for point B.

(5, 4)   (5, 1)   (4, 5)   (1, 5)

41 Join points ABC and then join C to A.
What shape have you drawn?

_____

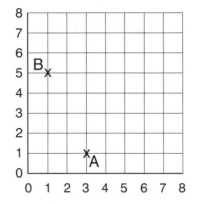

4

This graph shows the number of each type of pet that a vet saw in one month.

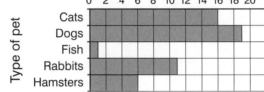

Animals visiting a vet

42 Which type of pet did the vet see the most? _____

43 Which type of pet did the vet see only one of? _____

44 How many more dogs than cats did the vet see? _____

45 How many hamsters and rabbits did the vet see in total? _____

4

46–49 Write the circled numbers in the correct place on the Carroll diagram.

X̶ 2̶ 3̶ 4̶ 5̶ 6̶ 7̶ 8̶ 9̶ 1̶0̶ ⑪ 1̶2̶ 1̶3̶ ⑭ 1̶5̶ 1̶6̶ 1̶7̶ 1̶8̶ 1̶9̶ 2̶0̶ ㉑ 2̶2̶ 2̶3̶ ㉔ 2̶5̶ 2̶6̶ 2̶7̶ 2̶8̶ 2̶9̶ 3̶0̶

	Even number	Not an even number
Multiple of 7	28	7
Not a multiple of 7	16 2 26 4 18 6 20 8 10 12 22 30	23 15 1 3 17 27 19 5 13 29 9 25

4

50 How many even numbers between 1 and 30 are not multiples of 7?

_____

1

Mixed paper 4

1–4 Write this set of decimals in order to make the number statement correct.

| 5.08 | 80.5 | 8.5 | 5.85 |

_____ < _____ < _____ < _____

Look at these decimal numbers.

| 29.7 | 52.3 | 64.9 | 13.5 |

5 What is the difference between the largest number and the smallest number? _____

6 What is the largest total that can be made from adding two of these numbers? _____

7 What is the smallest total that can be made from adding two of these numbers? _____

8 What is the smallest difference that can be made between two numbers? _____

There are 3 classes each with 30 children going on a school trip with 12 adults.

9 The children are divided equally between 2 buses and there will be 6 adults on each bus. The buses will have all their seats full.

How many seats are there on each bus? _____

10 The children are put into equal-sized groups with 2 adults looking after each group.

How many adults and children in total will there be in each group? _____

Choose **one** of these methods to calculate the answer.

11 $342 \times 6 =$ _____

| × | 300 | 40 | 2 |

6 [| |] → _____

$$\begin{array}{r} 3\,4\,2 \\ \times \quad 6 \\ \hline \\ \hline \end{array}$$

4

4

1

12 Complete this division.

$$4\overline{)953}$$

Are these statements 'true' or 'false'? Circle the answer for each.

13 A multiple of 3 is always an odd number.   **true   false**

14 A multiple of 4 is always an even number.   **true   false**

15 Write a number between 15 and 20 that is a factor of 36.

15 < _____ < 20

16 Here are all the pairs of factors for a number.

Write the number and complete the first pair of factors.

_____ → (1, _____)   (2, 30)   (3, 20)   (4, 15)   (5, 12)   (6, 10)

17–20 Write these fractions in order, starting with the smallest.

$\frac{11}{20}$ $\frac{3}{5}$ $\frac{1}{2}$ $\frac{9}{10}$ _____   _____   _____   _____

21 What is the missing number in this sequence?

25   36   49   _____   81

22–23 Write the missing numbers in this sequence.

771   767   _____   759   _____   751

24 What is the next number in this sequence?   36   49   64   81   _____

Write **always**, **sometimes** or **never** to make each statement true.

25 Quadrilaterals _____ have 4 right angles.

26 A triangle _____ has parallel sides.

27 Cuboids _____ have 12 edges.

28 A triangular prism _____ has 6 faces.

29 What is the area of a square with 5 m sides?

Area   =   _____

30 What is the perimeter of a square with 10 cm sides?

Perimeter   =   _____

1

2

1

1

4

4

4

2

31–32 Complete this table.

	Length	Width	Area	Perimeter
Rectangle A	4 m	_____	20 square metres	18 m
Rectangle B	3 m	_____	21 square metres	20 m

2

33 Use a ruler to measure this line. Write your answer in millimetres.

├─────────────────────────────┤   _____ mm

1

34 Write the time shown on this clock. _____

35 What time will it be in 45 minutes? _____

2

36 Write the weight shown on these scales. _____

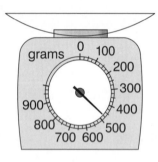

1

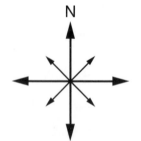

37 Label the arrow pointing W.

38 Label the arrow pointing NE.

39 Label the arrow pointing SW.

3

40 Draw a cross at point (0, 7) and label it A.

41 Draw a cross at point (3, 2) and label it B.

42 Draw a cross at point (5, 0) and label it C.

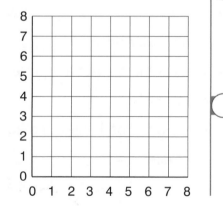

3

This graph shows the amount of rain for each month.

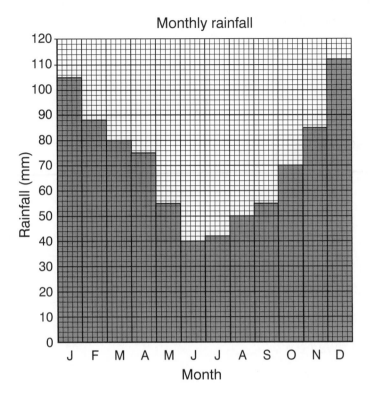

Monthly rainfall

43 Which month had 42 mm of rain? _____

44 Which month had the same amount of rain as September?

_____

45 How much more rain was there in March than June? _____

46 How many months had more than 60 mm of rain? _____

4

47–50 Write each circled letter in the correct place on the Venn diagram.

Ⓐ B Ⓒ Ⓓ E F G H I J K L M N O P Q R Ⓢ T U V W X Y Ⓩ

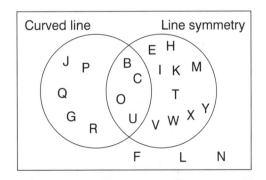

4

Mixed paper 5

Round each of these numbers to the nearest 100.

1 9090 _____

2 9009 _____

3 9909 _____

4 9990 _____

⟨4⟩

Complete these subtractions.

5
```
  7 1 0 5
-   9 7 6
---------

---------
```

6
```
  8 3 2 4
- 1 8 1 7
---------

---------
```

⟨2⟩

7 What is 13.7 added to 25.4? _____

8 What is 550 more than 2680? _____

9 What is 14.5 take away 6.4? _____

10 What is 220 less than 2000? _____

⟨4⟩

11 What is 27 multiplied by 18? _____

Use this grid to help you calculate the answer.

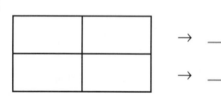

→ _____

→ _____

Total: _____

⟨1⟩

12 Complete this multiplication.

```
    3 5 6
×     4
---------

---------
```

13 Complete this division. $6\overline{)858}$

⟨2⟩

14 What is the remainder when 73 is divided by 5? _____

15 What is the smallest number that is a multiple of both 4 and 6? _____

⟨2⟩

16 Circle the number that is a multiple of both 3 and 7.

$$24 \quad 9 \quad 42 \quad 49 \quad 14$$

17–18 Write the missing factors for 28.

$$28 \quad \rightarrow \quad (1, 28) \quad (2, \_\_) \quad (4, \_\_)$$

19 What fraction of this shape is shaded? _____

20 Write 20% as a fraction in its lowest form. _____

21 Write $\frac{1}{4}$ as a percentage. _____

22 What is $\frac{1}{8}$ of 24? _____

Look at these number patterns. Write the next two numbers in each pattern.

23–24 16.6   16.1   15.6   _____   _____

25–26 4457   5457   6457   _____   _____

Look at this shape and answer the questions.

27 What is the name of this shape? _____

28 How many pairs of parallel lines are there in this shape? _____

29 How many right angles are there in this shape? _____

30 How many lines of symmetry does this shape have? _____

31 What is the perimeter of a swimming pool that is 4 m wide and 7 m long? _____

32 What is the area of a book cover that is 20 cm wide by 30 cm long? Underline the correct answer.

         50 square centimetres   60 square centimetres

               100 square centimetres

        500 square centimetres   600 square centimetres

33–34 What are the area and perimeter of this rectangle?

Area = _____

Perimeter = _____

6 m

11 m

1

2

4

4

4

2

2

41

35 What is the total weight of these boxes? _____kg _____g

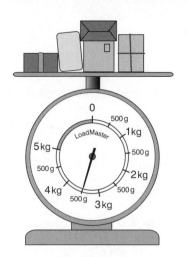

36 The boxes are all the same weight. What is the weight of one box?

_____

2

37 A cake was put in the oven at 2:55 and took 25 minutes to cook.

At what time was the cake ready to come out of the oven? _____:_____

1

38 What is 40 mm added to 25 cm? Write the answer in centimetres. _____

1

39–42 Complete this chart to show where you would be facing after each turn.

Start position, facing:	Turn	End position, now facing:
East	$\frac{1}{4}$ turn anticlockwise	_____
North	$\frac{1}{4}$ turn clockwise	_____
East	$\frac{1}{2}$ turn clockwise	_____
South	$\frac{1}{4}$ turn anticlockwise	_____

4

This block graph shows how many birds visited a bird table each morning and afternoon for five days.

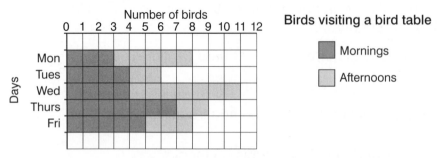

Birds visiting a bird table

■ Mornings
□ Afternoons

43 How many birds visited the bird table in total on Tuesday? _____

44 How many birds visited the bird table on Monday afternoon? _____

45 How many more birds visited the bird table on Thursday morning than on Thursday afternoon? _____

46 How many birds visited the bird table in total over these five days?

_____

47–50 Write the letters for each shape A–D in the correct position on the Carroll diagram.

A   B   C   D

	One or more acute angles	No acute angles
Quadrilateral	_____	_____
Not a quadrilateral	_____	_____

4

Now go to the Progress Chart to record your score!   Total   50

Mixed paper 6

These are some important dates in the development of communication.

Date	Communication development
1993	'www' was released for public use on the internet
1876	first successful telephone transmission
1929	first regular television broadcasts
1901	first successful transatlantic radio communication

1–4 Write the dates in order, starting with the earliest date.

_____   _____   _____   _____

earliest

5 How many years are there between the first successful telephone transmission and the first regular television broadcasts? _____ years

5

6 A fence is put around a playground. Two sides are 25.8 m and the other two sides are 17.4 m.

What is the total length of fence used for the playground? _____ ◯ 1

7–9 The digits 3, 4 and 5 are missing. Complete the addition with the digits in the correct place.

$$
\begin{array}{r}
\square\,4\ 7 \\
+\ 2\ 9\,\square \\
\hline
8\,\square\,0
\end{array}
$$

◯ 3

10 Which number between 30 and 40 has a remainder of 4 when it is divided by 8? _____ ◯ 1

11 A rabbit eats 80 g of food a day.

Would there be enough in a 560 g bag of food to feed the rabbit for a week?

Circle the answer: **yes**   **no** ◯ 1

12 Multiply 39 by 25. _____

13 Divide 908 by 7. _____ ◯ 2

14–17 Write each of these numbers in the correct part of the Venn diagram.

| 9 | 15 | 30 | 54 |

Factor of 45   Multiple of 5

◯ 4

18–19 Circle the two fractions that are greater than $\frac{1}{2}$

$\frac{5}{8}$ $\frac{1}{3}$ $\frac{5}{12}$ $\frac{3}{5}$ $\frac{3}{8}$ ◯ 2

20 Use two of these digits to make a fraction equal to $\frac{1}{4}$

| 2 | 3 | 4 | 7 | 8 |

$\frac{\square}{\square}$ ◯ 1

44

21 Circle the largest number.

22–23 Write the missing numbers in this sequence.

_____   150   300   600   _____

24 What is the next number in this sequence?

36   25   16   9   _____

25 What is the first number in this sequence?

_____   43   58   73   88   103

26–29 Write the letter for each shape in the correct position on the Carroll diagram.

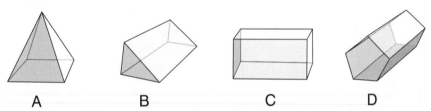

A   B   C   D

	Odd number of vertices	Even number of vertices
One or more triangular faces	_____	_____
No triangular faces	_____	_____

30 What is the perimeter of this shape?

_____

31 What is the area of this shape? Underline the answer.

100 square centimetres

84 square centimetres

80 square centimetres

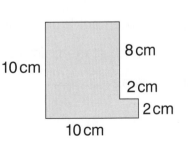

32 A classroom needs a new carpet. The room is 12m long and 9m wide.

What is the area of the classroom? _____

33 A square has an area of 4 square metres.

Circle the length of the perimeter of this square.

2m   4m   6m   8m

34–35 Circle the smallest quantity. Underline the greatest quantity.

5ml   6 litres   560ml   65ml   50 litres   600ml

36 How many grams are there in two and a half kilograms? _____ g

These 6 containers hold 27 litres in total when they are full. Each bottle holds 2 litres.

37 How much does each bucket hold? _____

38 Write the coordinates for point A.

(_____ , _____)

39 Draw a cross at point (3, 4) and label it B.

40 If you are standing at point A facing towards point B, are you facing north, south, east or west?

_____

41 Is this statement 'true' or 'false'? Circle the answer.

If you stand at the point (5, 3) and look north, you are facing point A.

true   false

2

2

1

1

4

This graph shows how many children there are in a number of families.

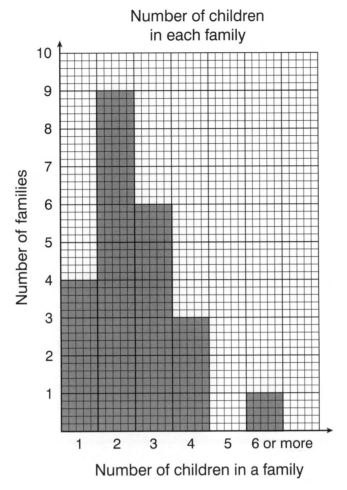

Number of children
in each family

Number of families

Number of children in a family

42 How many families have one child? _____

43 There are nine families with the same number of children.

How many children are there in each of these families? _____

44 How many families have four or more children? _____

45 All the families with three children meet for a picnic.

How many children are there in total at the picnic? _____

4

47

46–49 Write each of the circled numbers in the correct place on the Venn diagram.

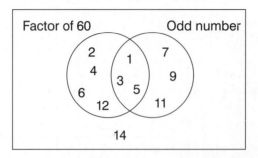

50 Write 30 in the correct section of the Venn diagram.

Now go to the Progress Chart to record your score!   Total ◯ 50

◯ 5